LEAVES FALL DOWN

Learning about Autumn Leaves

PICTURE WINDOW BOOKS
a capstone imprint

by Lisa Bullard

illustrated by Nadine Takvorian

Special thanks to our adviser for his expertise:

Terry Flaherty, PhD, Professor of English
Minnesota State University, Mankato

Shelly Lyons, editor; Lori Bye, designer
Nathan Gassman, art director; Jane Klenk, production specialist
The illustrations in this book were created digitally and with pencil.

Picture Window Books
151 Good Counsel Drive
P.O. Box 669
Mankato, MN 56002-0669
877-845-8392
www.capstonepub.com

Printed in the United States of America in North Mankato, Minnesota.
032010   005740CGF10

All books published by Picture Window Books
are manufactured with paper containing at least
10 percent post-consumer waste.

Library of Congress Cataloging-in-Publication Data
Bullard, Lisa.
Leaves fall down : learning about autumn leaves / by Lisa Bullard ;
illustrated by Nadine Takvorian.
p. cm. — (Autumn)
Includes index.
ISBN 978-1-4048-6013-1 (library binding)
ISBN 978-1-4048-6390-3 (paperback)
1. Defoliation—Juvenile literature. 2. Leaves—Juvenile literature.
3. Autumn—Juvenile literature. I. Takvorian, Nadine. II. Title. III.
Series: Autumn (Series)
QK763.B85 2010
581.4'8—dc22   2010000903

Hot summer days are gone.
The air is cooler now.
Winter will be here soon.
But first the trees put
on a colorful show.

Let's go for a walk.

Cool! Let's check
out the leaves.

3

All summer long, leaves soak up sunlight.
They are green and tender.

Some leaves are still holding on to the branches.

This one is still green.

5

The green color comes from chlorophyll.

Leaves need sunlight and chlorophyll
to make food for the trees.

Leaves work hard all summer long.
But why do trees lose their leaves?

When fall comes, there is less sunlight. Without as much sunlight, the leaves can't make food.

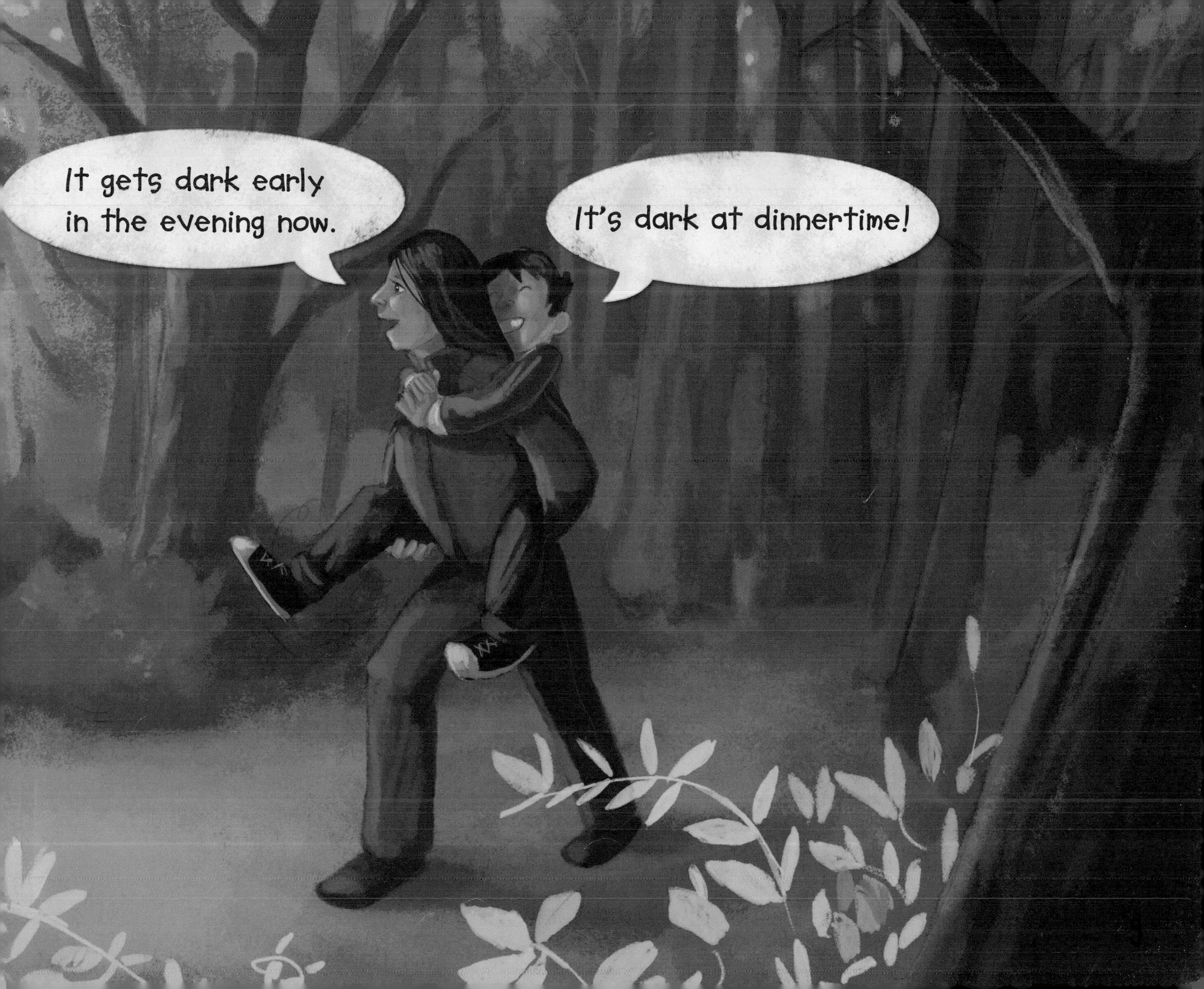
It gets dark early in the evening now.
It's dark at dinnertime!

The chlorophyll in the leaves disappears.
The leaves lose their green color.

This one's yellow.

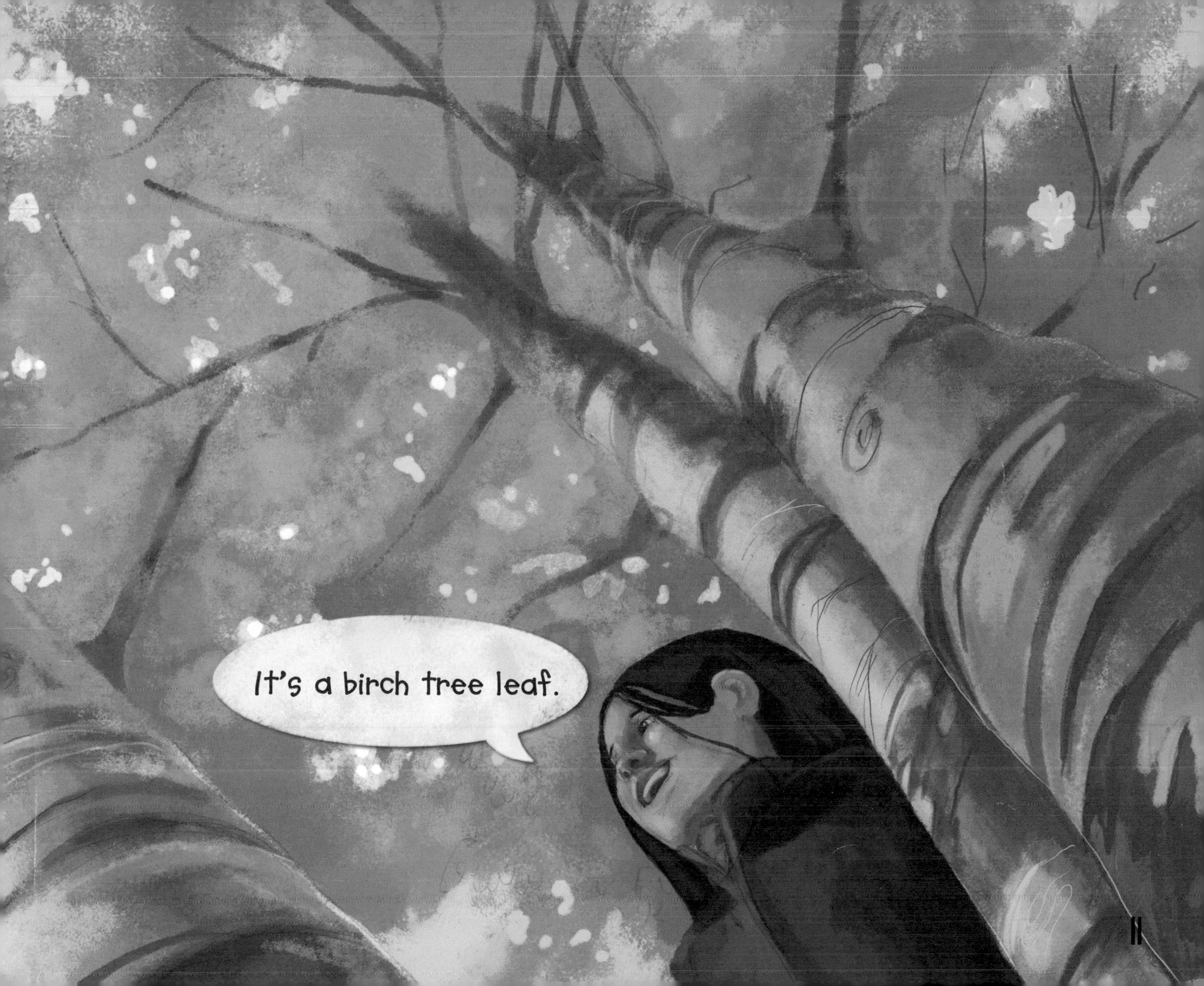
It's a birch tree leaf.

Bright colors have been hiding under the green.

The yellow color was in these leaves all along.

But we couldn't see it.

The leaves show their colors. Then they dry up.

Finally the leaves fall from the trees.

I get it! Leaves fall during fall, right?

With their leaves gone, the trees' branches are ready for winter.

That's right. We also call this time of year autumn.

Over time, the fallen leaves will mix with the soil.
The leaves make the soil rich for the trees.

Do we have to go home?
It's getting late. And tomorrow we need to check out our own leaves.

People often rake leaves to keep their yards tidy.

Some people put leaves into a compost bin. In spring, they mix the compost with soil to help plants grow.

But before getting rid of all the leaves, people make piles.
Then comes the best part of fall!

21

Leaves Window Art

What you need:

- clear contact paper
- a collection of colorful leaves
- 6 inches (15 centimeters) of ribbon
- scissors

What you do:

1. Cut a rectangular piece of contact paper.
   The piece should be twice as large as you want the window art to be.
2. Peel off the backing from the contact paper.
3. On half of the contact paper, arrange the leaves however you want.
4. Form a letter C with the ribbon. Fix each end of the "C" to the top edge of the contact paper, on the same half as the leaves. This will form a loop from which to hang the piece.
5. Fold the bare half of the contact paper over the half with the leaves.
6. Using the scissors, trim the edges so they aren't ragged.
7. Hang the piece against a window.

Glossary

autumn—the season of the year between summer and winter; autumn is also called fall

chlorophyll—the green matter in plants that uses light to make food

compost—a mixture of rotted leaves, vegetables, and other items that are added to soil to make it richer

tender—soft

More Books to Read

McNamara, Margaret. *Fall Leaf Project.* New York: Aladdin Paperbacks, 2006.

Rawlinson, Julia. *Fletcher and the Falling Leaves.* New York: Greenwillow Books, 2006.

Stein, David Ezra. *Leaves.* New York: G. P. Putnam's Sons, 2007.

Wallace, Nancy Elizabeth. *Leaves! Leaves! Leaves!* Tarrytown, N.Y.: Marshall Cavendish Children, 2007.

Internet Sites

FactHound offers a safe, fun way to find Internet sites related to this book. All of the sites on FactHound have been researched by our staff.

Here's all you do:
Visit *www.facthound.com*
FactHound will fetch the best sites for you!

Index

Check out all the books in the Autumn series:

Apples, Apples Everywhere!: Learning about Apple Harvests

Busy Animals: Learning about Animals in Autumn

Leaves Fall Down: Learning about Autumn Leaves

Pick a Perfect Pumpkin: Learning about Pumpkin Harvests